Things My Grandmother Told Me *of Yesterday*

HUGH H. HARDWICKE III

KWE PUBLISHING

Hardwicke III, Hugh H. *Things My Grandmother Told Me of Yesterday*

Copyright © 2024 by Hugh H. Hardwicke III all rights reserved.

ISBNs: 979-8-9906169-0-5 (paperback), 979-8-9906169-2-9 (hardcover), 979-8-9906169-1-2 (e-book)

I would like to acknowledge my grandmother, Eppes Hatcher Hardwicke, for telling us the stories of her life growing up on Hatcher's Island on the James River here in Virginia.

It is in reverence to her that I pass these stories along in a short book so that the children of today can read about what it was like to grow up during that period in life in Virginia.

I would also like to acknowledge my sister, Jan Hardwicke Cole, for the stories she shared with me.

Lastly, I would like to thank my wife, Lynne O'Bryan Hardwicke, for her untiring help editing this book and keeping me sane through the process of getting this compiled book of stories completed.

Introduction

The stories represented here are from the early 1900s when my grandmother, Eppes Hatcher Hardwicke, was a young girl living on Hatcher's Island on the James River in Virginia. These stories she shared with us sitting on the front porch of her house in Westmoreland County, Virginia, in the early days of our lives mattered so much and are so relevant to how they helped us grow up.

I trust the adults and children who will read these stories benefit from them as we did, and I hope that they find themselves entertained and want to look into their own family histories.

Camping

I remember my grandmother told me once that she, her sister, Elsie, her brother, Randolph, and her cousins often camped on the farm. Her parents would set up this big canvas tent and they would all get their blankets, collect up some straw, make their beds, and camp out. They would spend hours lolling in the nice green grass of the pasture, picking buttercups, and talking and laughing together.

One of these times, my aunt Elsie was sleeping with the rest of the kids in the tent. It was around early morning, and she heard this noise by her ear. She was scared to death and didn't know what it was. She let out a scream and jumped up—only to find a cow had his head in the tent, eating the hay that she had used to make her bed. She said she never liked cows after that.

Another time, my aunt, Elsie, was walking along the edge of the field that they were camped in, with all her cousins and brother and sister, and she looked up and saw this cow walking beside her. Well, being afraid of cows, she got scared and started running, and then, so did the cow. She ran even faster, and so did the cow.

Everybody was laughing at her, but she continued to run until she came to the end of the field and the fence and could run no more. Mostly out of breath, she sat down and started to cry.

All the others came up to her, still laughing, and said, "Don't be afraid, the cow is on the other side of the fence! There's no use in being scared. She can't get to you!"

Elsie still did not like cows.

An Uncle on Horseback

Grandmother's uncle would "tie one on," or "get tight," as grandmother would say, and climb on his big white horse and ride around the house.

One time, he rode his horse up on the porch, through the front door, and down the "dog trot" that separated the house in half. The dog trot was a long hallway that went between the two downstairs portions of the house. It had a screen door on the front and on the back.

Well, grandmother's mother would yell at him, "Get that horse out of here!" He would just ignore her and keep riding.

Soon, she got frustrated and went and got the broom, and when he came through again, it was his last ride through the house. She smacked at him, knocking him off the back of the horse and smartly to the ground. Flat on his back!

I don't ever remember her telling of a repeat performance by him, so it must have made a big impression on him.

Doing Your Schoolwork

After the evening meal, the school-age children would set about preparing themselves to study their lessons for school the next day. If it was during the winter months, oil lamps would have to be filled with lamp oil and lit. Usually, the big round oak table in the dining area was the scene for this work.

Each child had his or her special spot that they would occupy and would spread their schoolbooks and papers out in front of them. There was to be no talking unless it pertained to the chores at hand. The children's grandmother was usually handy to administer any disciplinary actions required, which were very few. Folks of those times understood and took seriously the learning process and yearned for every bit of knowledge that could be had, whether it be from books or from the experiences of the older residents of the household.

When all were through with their lessons, it was off to bed.

During the winter, it was customary to place your "bed brick" on the hearth, next to the fire, before you started your lessons.

Upon completion of your schoolwork, you fetched your brick and wrapped it in a small piece of wool blanket that had been specifically cut from an old blanket for you to place your brick in. You then used the outhouse and were off to your room, where you placed your brick under the covers at the foot of the bed. This would help keep your feet warm for a while, allowing you to get to sleep quicker. All in a day's work for the children during those times.

William Green Hall

"These were a hardy and brave lot, and they meant to give the Yankee commander a run for his money," my grandmother would say about my great-great-great grandfather, William Green Hall, and his fellow soldiers.

William had served in the Confederate States Army during the War Between the States as a private in the 24th Virginia Cavalry. He enlisted in Richmond around the spring of 1862 and served until the end of the war, May 1865. He was a courier for generals Beauregard, Magruder, and Lee. William had a stomach ailment that kept him from performing his duties in the infantry. He was transferred to the cavalry around late 1862, where he made the famous ride around General McClellan with General Jeb Stuart and soon-to-be Captain Robins. Captain Robins commanded the 24th Virginia Cavalry upon its re-organization.

"They were all excellent horsemen and knew the countryside they were traveling," my grandmother would add.

These young men, most of whom were in their early twenties, and by today's standards, were a very daring and reckless breed. They completed their little jaunt, as history proves, and lived to tell about it.

I was given a Confederate "Virginia" uniform button that belonged to my great-great-great-grandfather, as well as his parole slip, a one-hundred-dollar bill that was issued to him, and the stamped envelope that he sent it home in. These documents hang on my bedroom wall, nicely framed and protected from the elements.

Going to Stay with Cousins in Chester

During the summer months, when the mosquitoes were at their worst, the family would move up to Chester, away from the river, and stay with their cousins at their big farmhouse. There were no such things as screen windows and screened doors in these times. They had not been invented yet. The mosquitoes reproduced quickly along the river's edge and low grounds around the farm.

Staying with the cousins was the highlight of the summer. It was like being on vacation—or better. There were new stories to listen to and new things to try. It was like the first day of school. Such excitement!

After the novelty wore off, which was usually in a couple of days, it took a lot of imagination to keep oneself occupied and out of trouble, whether they were inside playing or outside. The boys would pit themselves against the girls and vice versa. There were more girls than boys, so the girls would fend off most of the boys' attacks. Everyone tried to stay outside because the temperature was cooler. It didn't take long for the adults to tire of such foolishness and find some constructive work for those who continued to "act up."

Of course, there was summer vacation Bible school to beat the humdrums for a couple of weeks. This was always looked forward to. There were lots of crafts for the kids to do, and of course, the Bible study would prove to be the major highlight of the term. Upon graduation, each child would receive a "diploma" for their efforts during the week.

A trip to the general store was another way to pass away the hours. The kids hurried into the store, staring at the large strings of licorice that could be bought for a penny, as well as maybe the apples or peaches if they happened to be in season.

A look through the ladies' catalog by the girls was the main topic of discussion, and all the young ladies were anxious to breeze through it the first chance they had. Looking through the latest patterns was another must-do.

After returning to the farm in the wagon, there was much chatter. The young ladies excitedly talked about the newest fabrics available in the store and their ideas for a new dress or bonnet for church, made with cool fabrics for summer. There was much fuss by the others as to what clothes would be made and from which materials. Others were more concerned by things such as the weather and who was going to the church social that afternoon. Everyone was excited for summer to begin.

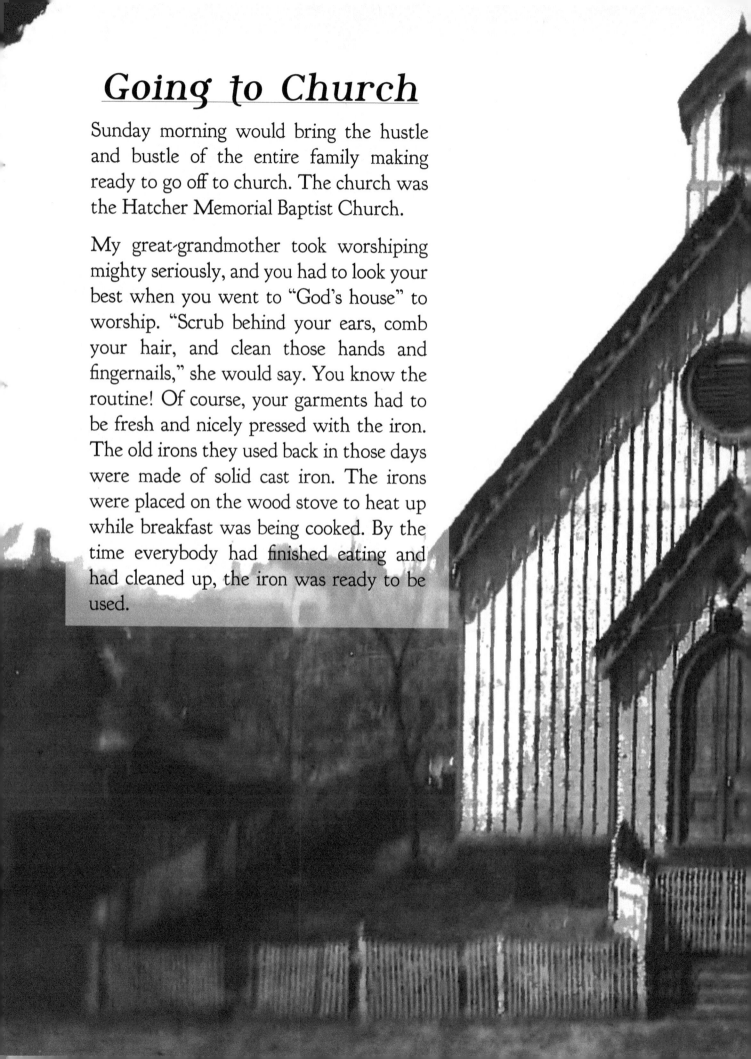

Going to Church

Sunday morning would bring the hustle and bustle of the entire family making ready to go off to church. The church was the Hatcher Memorial Baptist Church.

My great-grandmother took worshiping mighty seriously, and you had to look your best when you went to "God's house" to worship. "Scrub behind your ears, comb your hair, and clean those hands and fingernails," she would say. You know the routine! Of course, your garments had to be fresh and nicely pressed with the iron. The old irons they used back in those days were made of solid cast iron. The irons were placed on the wood stove to heat up while breakfast was being cooked. By the time everybody had finished eating and had cleaned up, the iron was ready to be used.

My great-grandpa went to the barn and hooked up Old Mag to the buggy that was used to transport the family to the church. It would take an hour and a few minutes to arrive.

When everyone was loaded on board, the old bay strained at the leathers and started off for church.

Upon reaching the church grounds, Great-grandpa would look for a big tree with plenty of shade to park Old Mag under while the family was in the chapel. See, you didn't leave your horse, or your mule, for that matter, out in the sun. It would make them sick. You needed those animals to make your living and provide for your family, so you took care of them. You had to water them also, so a bucket was usually attached to the rear of the buggy or wagon. This way, you always had a refreshing drink for them when you reached your destination.

After church, there was time for the grownups to talk, and the children ran and played around the church grounds for a while. Then, everyone loaded up in the buggy again and headed home.

Once home, the women set about making the noon meal, which usually consisted of a baked chicken, or two, depending on who was coming for dinner. Fresh vegetables were on the list, too, if they were in season, with hot rolls and maybe a freshly baked apple pie. There was also plenty of tea and lemonade.

After eating, the family would gather outside under the shade of the walnut trees to sit and talk and enjoy each other's company.

Kiss-Me-Kate at the Garden Gate

There was a little blue flowering bush, called "Kiss-Me-Kate," that grew on the arched fence in the front yard of the house on Coxendale Road, leading to Hatcher's Island. The story goes that the bush was put there, sort of like when you would hang mistletoe over the door at Christmas time. To steal a kiss from your boyfriend or girlfriend! Well, when the girls brought their boyfriends home, they could use the Kiss-Me-Kate bush to ensure they would get a kiss from their "beau."

Making Ice Cream

The children would all gather around the back porch of the Hatcher House when one of the ladies of the house would announce, "We are going to make ice cream soon!" First, the big wooden bucket with its canister would have to be fetched by one of the boys. When the salt and the ice had been added to the outside, the canister with the cream and fruit would be inserted. Then, the kids would take turns turning the handle that would soon produce the peach or raspberry ice cream (or whatever the desired flavor had been concocted for their hungry little appetites).

All this took a little time, and, of course, everyone wanted to have a turn at the handle so that they could say that they had helped make the cream. Soon, the cream was ready to be scooped out. Everyone was given a big bowl of fresh fruity delicacy to eat in the shade of the big walnut trees that grew in the yard around the house.

The Pocahontas

All the kids and cousins were fishing and swimming in the river by the rocks when a big paddle boat, Pocahontas, tried to make the turn and ran aground. My grandmother ran to the house, which was just a short way away from where they were swimming, and got her father. Being out of breath from running, she tried to tell her father about the boat on the river but found it difficult to say anything right away.

Finally, she caught her breath and said, "There's a boat stuck at the rocks!" He immediately went and fetched his mules and walked them to the river's edge to see what he could do to help the captain get his boat off the rocks. There was nothing that could be done, for the tide was out, and they would have to wait until the water came in to help get them freed.

In the meantime, the captain gave all the kids a tour of the large paddle boat, taking them to the helm and letting them touch the big wheel that guided the boat up and down the river. They were very excited and had lots to talk about for many days afterward.

Several hours later, the tide came in. The captain started up the large steam-driven motors that powered the paddle wheels. He put the wheels in reverse to try and back off the rocks. After much struggling, the boat soon broke free and backed away, getting back on track for the journey down the river.

For many years, the ships went up and down the river, and to my knowledge, there were never any more incidents of any of the other ships getting stuck. The kids ran along the bank, waving at the boats as they made their way up and down the James River.

The Buttercup and Cicadas

Growing amongst the other weeds in the cow pasture is the little buttercup, a yellow flower that has several blooms on a long stem. Cows eat them, and they shed their beautiful yellow glow over the fields in abundance during the spring.

My grandmother used to tell me that if you picked one and held it up under your chin, it glowed a bright yellow glow.

After the buttercups in the spring, summer came. On hot summer afternoons, we would take mid-afternoon naps (usually in our rooms, but sometimes in another place of our choosing, such as the front porch). We could always hear the ever-present buzz of the cicadas up in the treetops and tree limbs. Yes, the locusts! I am not sure if they are the same thing that is talked about in the Bible or not, but we were not afraid of them. They just hung around and made a soothing buzzing noise with their legs and wings that sometimes would put us to sleep.

The insects were a feast to the mockingbirds, which hunted them down and devoured each and every one it would catch. As kids, we watched the tree trunks for the thin brown shells that they would shed and leave behind, clutching to the bark of all the trees for miles around.

The Oil Lamp in the Parlor

Grandmother's older sister, Stanley, would always bring her boyfriend to the house after their dates. They would sit in the parlor and "talk." There was an oil lamp that hung in the center of the room from the ceiling, and it could be raised up or down to light it. Stanley would like it a little darker so she and her boyfriend could "talk," so she would pull the lamp down and blow it out. The lamp was on a chain that would squeak when you lowered or raised it, and it was noticeable to anyone in the house.

Stanley's mother, hearing the lamp squeak, knew what was going on. She would say to one of the younger girls, "Go downstairs and re-light the lamp."

After several times, Grandmother said she was too embarrassed to go back down and re-light the lamp. Great-grandmother would finally have to go downstairs and say something to Stanley, for she did not approve of youngsters "talking in the dark."

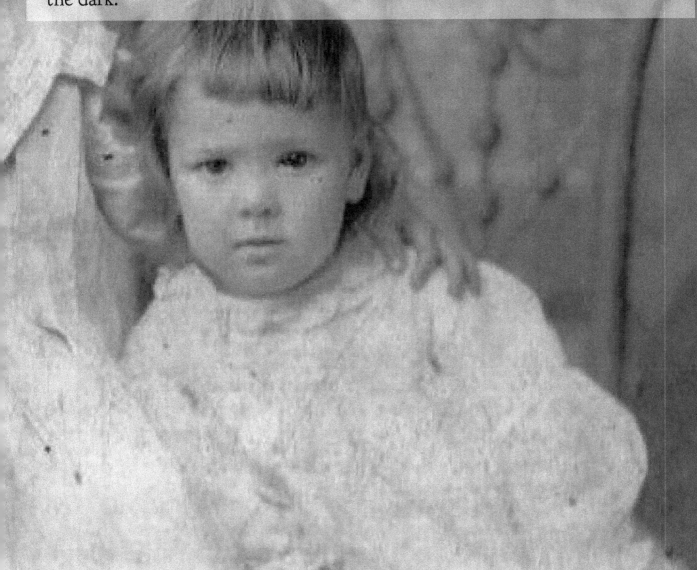

Whippoorwills

Many a summer evening was spent on the front porch swing listening to the "whippoorwills," and his cousin, the "poorwills," as they answered each other back and forth through the woods. The whippoorwill makes a strange sound, to say the least. These little birds, common only at night, are very solitary, nocturnal, and evasive and seem to call their loud, repeated call, suggestive of their name, for a mate out of the darkness.

If you were not aware of what it was, you may even be afraid of them. But no one after identification has been made could ever be afraid of this timid and secretive creature. It is another one of God's great creations. We would sit and swing, listening to them whistle their song long into the evening.

Trip to Buckroe Beach

When Grandmother was in high school, the church group would charter the train in Richmond and take a day trip to Buckroe Beach. There was the beach to enjoy and an amusement park, at which you could ride the amusement rides, and of course the water at the beach.

One Sunday, Grandmother was in a new white dress and decided to ride the merry-go-round. There was a gold ring that hung on one of the outside posts, and the goal was to reach way out and grab it as your pony rounded by. Well, Grandmother was reaching for the ring, and she reached a little too far, and she slipped right off the back of her merry-go-round pony. She shot right out onto the dirt and messed up her pretty new dress.

"Oh, I've ruined my new dress," she cried. "Don't laugh at me," she told her friends. "Grandmother is going to skin my hide!"

Box Turtle

Grandmother, her brother, and her sisters would keep an eye open in the spring of every year for a box turtle to keep all summer long as a pet. It would spend the summer up in a wooden corral in the backyard under a shaded tree. The kids would take turns catching insects and feeding the turtle.

At the end of the summer, they were released back to Mother Nature to return to their normal routines and habitats. Sometimes, the turtle would just hang around like a stray dog might, waiting to be fed by the kids.

The kids were sad to see it go, but if they were lucky, it would return the following year.

That Old Gray Horse

Grandmother's father would ride his old horse in from working in the fields. One day, there was a real bad thunderstorm with lightning and thunder.

While my great-grandfather was riding his horse on this day, a lightning bolt shot across the field, toward my great-grandfather's head. The old horse stooped down just in time, and the lightning bolt struck through his straw hat, knocking it to the ground and scaring Great-grandfather.

Coincidence or not, my great-grandfather thought he was rather lucky that day and very lucky to have that old gray horse.

Mount Hope

Mount Hope is a little cottage on top of a hill in Chesterfield County, Virginia. The home was built in 1834, and the land it is on was given to William Hatcher in 1740 by King George II of England.

I went to the house when I was eleven or twelve years old. As a child, I thought the house was a huge mansion.

I remember two little ladies, the Gregory sisters, who lived in the house. That day we visited, one of the Gregory sisters came to the front door and opened it, and out stuck a barrel of a rifle!

My dad quickly told her who we were and that we were from the area, saying we wanted to see the house.

She relaxed and said, "Oh, well come in the house!"

Inside the house, there was crystal and glassware everywhere. It was fancy, though it hadn't always been that way.

Mount Hope is made of mostly pine wood and put together with wooden pegs. It had two large brick chimneys in the main house and a chimney in each of the other rooms, which were used to heat the house in winter. In 1858, William Hatcher had a kitchen built with an unfinished attic joined to the house. In 1950, the Gregorys finally added a new bath with all-new plumbing and electrical wiring throughout.

The house was used as a field hospital and temporary headquarters by General Benjamin Butler of the Union Army during the Civil War. When the house was under construction in the 1960s, my father and I explored the trenches, which were still there from the Civil War. We found artifacts from the war all along the ditch.

The house remained in the Hatcher-Gregory family until 1990. Florence and Elizabeth, the Gregory sisters, lived in the house until they were unable to care for themselves.

Over the many years, several families lived and loved in Mount Hope. Though time has passed, the house still stands, representing many years of love and history.

Acknowledgment

I would like to acknowledge my Grandmother Eppes Hatcher Hardwicke for telling us the stories of her life growing up on Hatchers Island on the James River here in Virginia. It is in reverence to her that I pass these along in a short book so that the children of today can read about what it was like to grow up during that period in life in Virginia.

I would also like to acknowledge my sister Jan Hardwicke Cole for the stories she gave me.

About the Author

Hugh was born and raised in Chesterfield, Virginia. Almost every Sunday, he and his family went to his grandmother's house to visit. She told stories to him and his siblings and taught him to paint artistically. After he grew up, he attended John Tyler Community College and Virginia Commonwealth University.

After living in Powhatan, Virginia, for twenty-nine years, Hugh and his wife, Lynne, moved back to Chesterfield for the last eleven years. They are both retired and enjoy visiting with family and researching information for his books.

Hugh has invested his time in many extra activities over the past several years, including hiking, camping, and fishing. Hugh enjoys indoor activities such as painting and recently, writing. He has collected much information on his ancestors and has compiled much of this information into a book of genealogy.